THE LEGACY SELLING SYSTEM

HOW TO CREATE MORE LEADS
BUILD DEEPER NETWORKS
AND CLOSE MORE DEALS

MICHEAL J. BURT

Murfreesboro, TN

Micheal Burt Enterprises
Murfreesboro, TN 37129

CoachBurt.com

Ordering Information:
Quantity sales. Special discounts may be available on quantity purchases by corporations, associations, and others. For details, info@coachburt.com.

The Legacy Selling System / Micheal Burt — 1st ed.
ISBN 978-0-578-66857-4

TABLE OF CONTENTS

*Dedicated to my amazing wife, Natalie,
for truly living with a Monster, and to
my little Monster, Ella Grace*

THE LEGACY SELLING SYSTEM

Welcome to the system that will move the needle in your business dramatically.

Before we dive in, let me ask you a question…

What if you had a selling system that radically increased your probability of getting in front of more people and closing more deals? A system that helped you build deep and meaningful relationships and attract the right people to you.

That's what I want to give to you in this short book; a true customer-getting strategy that moves your sales and business forward in a meaningful way.

Here's how It came about and what led me to create it for you.

For over a decade I was a high school basketball coach. I played the percentages and when we had less than 14 turnovers, gave up less than seven second shots, and stopped the other team 21 times in a game with a series of three consecutive stops, we won almost 90% of the time. It was a game of "systems" and "statistics." I always played the percentages because the percentages never lied to me and I don't believe in loving things that won't love you back.

The Law of Diffusion and Innovation rarely lies to me either, especially in selling. It tells me that when I present an idea (which is all selling really is) to another person, roughly 2.5% of the people will be "innovators." This means they will see it and most likely take action on it the first time they see it.

Roughly, an additional 13.5% of people are "early adopters," meaning they will have to see it one to three times before they take action. Once they see it a few times, though, there is a high "probability" that they will move.

That leaves 34% of the population that will be the "early majority." These are the people who will have to see the idea three to seven times before they take action.

Another 34% are called the "late majority" and will have to see the idea seven to 15 times before they act. Finally, about 16% of the population are "laggards" and they will *never* take action.

We test this model daily in my office on the number of calls we make, the number of ideas we present, and the percentage of people who take action on those ideas. Almost every time it is 16% (the "innovators" plus the "early adopters") on the dot.

This means that, if we make 30 phone calls and present 30 ideas to 30 different suspects (you'll see why I don't call them prospects later in the book), roughly 4.8 of those people will be interested in the idea we are presenting.

Selling, like winning a basketball game, is a game of probability. And I *always* play the percentages, because, remember, they don't lie to me (and they won't lie to you, either).

At 25 years old I wrote my first of 16 books and quickly began to build demand for my speaking and coaching business (which really wasn't even a business at the time) even while I was still coaching basketball. Every time I took action and spoke, I drove up the probability of creating more events. After all, money and opportunity always follow action, never stagnation.

After years of speaking and coaching business people alongside my basketball career, I won a championship at 31. I did it by playing the percentages and it created a national powerhouse.

I felt like I had "peaked" and realized I was bored and looking for my next adventure, so I started my business coaching businesses and salespeople. I would go out into the market and "look" for people who wanted my services.

I quickly figured out that, unlike my basketball coaching career, I didn't have a *system* to win. And winning in the business world is about one thing: *the creation of new customers and new money*.

See, I believe that most, if not all, of your days should be spent around generating new money for your business. The business people I was coaching were more lost than I was when it came to "customer acquisition." They didn't have a plan to get new customers that had more than two strategies.

Because of this, I quickly figured out that I needed to develop a system for myself that I could duplicate and use to help my clients. With the help and guidance of a small business coach (*everybody* needs a coach in life), I developed what would become the Legacy Selling System.

The Legacy Selling System is a CALCULATED and COORDINATED attack on new customer acquisition. It's a plan to circulate and CREATE new money for your business every single day.

While most selling systems teach you "what to say" when you get in front of people, they have a big missing structure: They don't teach you how to get in front of more prospects. And if you're not in front of prospects, it doesn't matter how good you are at "what to say."

When you work the Legacy Selling System, you can generate a significant number of new leads each month by combining the multiple strategies you'll learn in this book.

For my company, it has created as many as 1,000 leads per month by layering strategies on top of each other. This drives an incredible amount of new customer acquisition.

With the Legacy Selling System, every single week you have a "Hit List" of people to go after that you'd like to work with. You have interested prospects in your "Farm Club" and you seek out "Connectors" that have influence, all while loving on your "Top 25." You have new customers that you're turning into "Promoters and Advocates," and "Climbers" who form your future pipeline so you never run out. And you have a "Showcase" and "Database" to drive new business today.

The Hit List consists of people I have targeted and believe I can help with my services and I use it daily. This list is about *initiating* a meeting, a contact, a strategy, or an opening. It can consist of direct leads, current clients we are trying to "upsell" or generate a new lead from, past clients, or strategic partners. Every day I have a Hit List and I initiate. I cover the Hit List in Chapter One.

I layer other strategies on top of my Hit List (all of which you will learn). These include a Farm Club, a Top 25, Connectors, Climbers, Net Promoter, and one of my best strategies, the Showcase event.

These strategies all work in conjunction with each other. I map them out at the start of each week and I practice all of them *daily*. But the key is that I execute on them, and that is why I generate leads.

A lead is any person who has indicated interest in your product or service. They can come in the form of Instagram likes, LinkedIn messages, website hits, at event opt-ins, and more.

With seven billion people on planet Earth there is no shortage of leads, money, or opportunity. There is however a shortage of initiative, courage, and confidence. The Legacy Selling System gives you the tools to generate those leads (and the money and opportunity that come with them).

What the Legacy Selling System does is dramatically increase your probability of getting prospects and closing sales. It gives you the plan to *win*.

It gives you simple, yet valuable techniques to map out your days and go on offense, meaning spending most of your day going after new money. To make it work, though, you have to get clear on your time systems, which refers to how you spend the hours in your day.

Here's the time system we use in my office. Every morning we meet at 8:30 am to "pump the troops up" so we're ready to take on the day. From 9:00 am to 11:30 am we go into NEW MONEY cycles, focused completely on generating new business.

We break for lunch and then meet again to get fired up. (*Never* underestimate the need to re-enthuse your people). Then from 1:30 pm to 4:30 pm, we go back into NEW MONEY cycles again.

Why do we do this? Because we believe much of the day should be spent in HIGH VALUE ACTIVITY. High Value Activities are activities that generate new money. Too many companies I work with waste up to three to four hours per day in LOW VALUE ACTIVITY, which is non-money generating activity.

By giving yourself or your team a "time system," you eliminate the low value activity problem. After implementing this selling system, you can then "manage" to this system with your people.

Every day we are out there fishing. We can either fish for "blue gills," which are small fish that yield little return and little revenue, or we can fish for "blue marlins," which are big fish that yield much greater returns and have more influence to introduce us to other "blue marlins."

If done correctly, and you move the needle for your clients, each client should bring you as many as 5.7 more clients. This is where your Top 25 and Net Promoters come in, and you'll learn how to maximize these strategies in Chapters two and four.

My belief is that "every day with your current customer is an interview for your next customer." When you "move the needle" and a meaningful statistic in your current clients' lives and businesses, you'll be rewarded with more.

In the words of Wallace D. Wattles in *The Science of Getting Rich*, "And in so far as your business consists in dealing with other men, the key thought of all of your efforts must be to convey to their minds the impression of increase. Increase is what all men and all women are seeking."

When working this system of touches, follow ups, and bumps and nudges, always leave the other person with a feeling of "increase." A feeling that, in your care, they will expand.

This system will put you front of a lot – possibly thousands - of people daily and weekly. When people have this feeling about you, that you are a "person of advancement" and someone who can help them increase, they will gravitate toward you and want what you have. If a person believes you "advance" all those you come in contact with, then they will want to partner with you.

Selling is nothing more than presenting an idea that can solve a problem for another person by using your primary skill or the primary skill of the organization. The better you get at this, the more increase you will experience.

Now, it's time to increase your business to its fullest capacity by learning the nuts and bolts of this system.

CHAPTER 1

YOUR HIT LIST

The first step of the Legacy Selling System is to create a "Hit List." You can also think of it as your "Help List."

Simply put, your Hit List is all of the people you believe you can help with your products or services, with whatever you are selling. The Hit List initiates *everything*. If your pipeline is too minimal, it's for one reason; your Hit List is too minimal.

One of the questions I am asked most often in my coaching program, Monster Producers, is, "Where do the people on my Hit List come from?" The people on your Hit List can come from any of these four areas:

- Direct leads you are generating

- Current clients you want to generate new business with or get a referral from

- Past clients that may be attracted back based on pricing or new product offering (why having multiple products is so powerful)

- Strategic partners who, when you partner, create an increase for both of you

The Hit List is all about initiating. It's about seeing opportunity and reaching out to people to initiate that opportunity. When you come across people who could be interested in your product or services, or you can partner with you need to "initiate" a conversation or meeting to explore that possibility.

I would never come into a day without a Hit List. This is the starting point for everything. Let me give you a real-life example:

A few years back, I spoke at Grant Cardone's 10X Conference to over 10,000 people. I met many of the other speakers and found I had a particular affinity with some of them. I made contact with them and built relationships, which has led to me now doing events with these other big-time speakers.

These events have put me in front of all new people that end up on my Hit List. *This* is a Hit List activation. The Hit List kickstarts the entire system. It represents new opportunity for all the people you can help that may not know what you can offer them.

Each week, when you wake up and begin to move and circulate, you create *suspects*. I'm sure you've heard of *prospects* before, but suspects always come before prospects. We don't start with prospects (like many salespeople teach) for one simple reason: If I don't know what you do and why you matter, I can't be a prospect of yours!

As a buyer, I need to know how you can help me and, really, I need to know if you're an asset to me or a liability to me. Are you going to cost me money, time, or energy? Or are you going to make or save me money, time, or energy?

So when you think about this concept, your Hit List should be people that you would like to have a relationship with. People you think you could help with whatever you're selling and people you need to get in front of to make it happen.

We can't do business with a person until we get in front of them, and we can't get in front of them until we get their attention. Once we get their attention, we can articulate our value, we can let them know how we're a person of interest, we can turn them on to us. We can bring incredible energy to the equation.

A Hit List is an intentional way to say, "Every single week I wake up and I go after sales. I am not reactive. I'm not a secret agent - I don't sit in my office and wait for the phone to ring or for leads to come in. I am *intentional* about getting in front of people and creating opportunity."

Being intentional is how you sell and it's how you win.

I believe you should have a minimum of 25 people on your Hit List each week. More is OK, but NEVER less than 25.

Not everyone should be on your Hit List. You're only looking for what I call "ideal suspects." For each person you might put on your Hit List, you have to run them through your opportunity filter. Your opportunity filter is what you use to determine if someone would be a good fit for you. Your filter may be different than someone else's and it may be different than mine.

For example, my opportunity filter is this:

> *They have the time, the interest, and the money. They also are enlightened people who have a genuine desire to go to a new level in their businesses and their lives. They have a unique perspective versus a common perspective. I learn from them like they learn from me.*
>
> *We share a vested partnership - we are in this thing together. We both have skin in the game, which leads to collective passion.*
>
> *And when all these things check out, it forms a great relationship. They value and compensate me for my services and the value I create, and I take them to a higher level.*

Create your own opportunity filter and then build your Hit List with people you can get in front of and help. Sit down at night and map out 5-10 people you will be "hitting on" the next day. Based on this, every single week you should be cultivating a Hit List with a *minimum* of 25 people.

Reach out and get their attention through any means necessary. Call them, text them, email them, send them a video, etc. Make sure you have something valuable they want (access to networks, energy, skill sets, introductions, and more). If you aren't getting their attention, it's because they don't perceive what you have as valuable.

Never come into a day without this Hit List completed.

Once you have your Hit List, you get the attention of the people on it and share your Explanation of Value (EOV).

(Want to know more about structuring your EOV? Email info@coachburt.com and my team will share our process with you ASAP.)

CHAPTER 2

YOUR FARM CLUB

Once you have your Hit List and Top 25, it's time to cultivate your Farm Club. Your Farm Club is your list of *prospects* that you are trying to get to a buying decision.

The people on your Hit List are your suspects. You need to get in front of these people and articulate your value and explain to them why you "look different and run faster" than your competitors. You need to explain to them how you can help them move their "ball down the field." Once you do this and they indicate interest - they say they're interested in your services - you move them to your Farm Club.

Your Farm Club is a working list of prospects that have "raised their hands" and said, "I'm interested in what you have to offer." They are the people you are trying to close. You do that by cultivating the relationship and practicing an incredible 7-touch Follow-up. (For more on my 7-touch Follow-up, email info@coachburt.com and my team will get back to you right away).

Prospects who sit in your Farm Club are stalling you for some reason. It may be that money is a problem and they don't think they can afford it now or that it's not worth it. It could be you haven't done a good enough job articulating your value, or it could be they are trapped in the "current of the urgent." Whatever it is, there's a reason they aren't moving forward.

I use Newton's First Law to understand this. It states that an object at rest will stay at rest unless acted on by an outside force, just like an object in motion will stay in motion unless acted on by an outside force.

People in your Farm Club are at *rest*. They are "thinking on it," stalling, and they are *busy*. That's where you come in.

You've got to figure out a way to push them out of the Farm Club and into becoming clients. And you need to be creative with this.

You need to come up with creative emotional touches that get the prospect to say, "I'm ready to do this. Let's go." I call these touches the knockout punch and it's how you get somebody over the line. It's how you create a sense of urgency to say, "We've got to do this right now. It's so important and so vital to your future that we've got to do this right *now*."

You get your Farm Club moving *now* by coming up with 7-15 emotional touches. You have to connect with them in such a way that they simply can't stay "on the fence." We call these 7-15 touches "Million Dollar Follow-up." (To see how to get a personal copy of my book, *Million-Dollar Follow Up*, reach out to my team at info@coachburt.com now).

   THE LEGACY SELLING SYSTEM

Never forget your Farm Club is your Farm Club because they *indicated interest*. When you follow-up, you need to rekindle the initial fire you had that created that interest. Your job is to reach out and touch these people while creating a sense of urgency, and add unique value to get them across the finish line and become clients.

The Farm Club is about creating URGENCY. Imagine all the people who have indicated interest in your services that you have not closed. This number could be a very large number and it can represent a massive amount of opportunity.

There are two reasons people are not taking action in your Farm Club: fear and uncertainty. Fear is an unpleasant emotion that leads people to believe something is going to harm them in the future. It causes them to vacillate and waver back and forth. Ultimately, it breeds insecurity and inaction.

Because of this, the primary purpose of the Farm Club is to "feed the prospect information" and show them how you can solve their primary problem for them *better than anyone else* could.

Here is my current strategy for our Farm Club:

- Build an irresistible offer that creates a *sense of urgency* to take action on the spot

- Create a tight follow-up timeframe and begin your 7-touch follow-up system immediately

- Show the prospect how you will use your "methodology" to solve their greatest problem (Some call this a "Flash Roll" - taking something complicated and making it simple in a way that clearly demonstrates *you* are the expert)

- Use a series of both LINEAR (direct) and NON-LINEAR (indirect) touches in the follow up via different methods (phone call, email, voice text, video)

One of our best strategies in the follow-up are one-minute videos with voice-overs from me challenging the prospect to think about something in their business. This allows them to build an "affinity" with me so they can see we believe the same things, a requirement before they take action. *People do business with other people that believe the same things they do.*

Once the prospect believes you can solve their problem (based on your Flash Roll) and you are in alignment, they are closer to making a buying decision.

In my book *Million Dollar Follow Up,* I break down all of the challenge questions I use to bring a person to a buying decision. (Email my team at info@coachburt.com to find out how to get a copy). My main strategy is to show *absolute certainty* that I am uniquely qualified to solve their problem.

I believe the follow-up is one of the primary places people lose millions of dollars. They can't get and keep the attention of the prospect, which means they can't bring the buyer to a decision. Because of this, they don't follow-up after the sale either, and miss opportunities to further engage and get referrals.

The Farm Club is all about getting people who have indicated interest to take action and become clients. Once they're clients, they can feed you 5.7 referrals...IF you bring them onboard right and *turn them into advocates*.

CHAPTER 3

YOUR TOP 25

Once you have your Hit List, it's time to put together what I believe is the most important part of the Legacy Selling System: Your Top 25.

If you came to me and asked me which strategy you could use to generate the most money in the entire selling system, I would tell you it's the Top 25. These are 25 people who love and respect you, who advocate for you, who promote you and become "feeder systems" for you. This strategy alone could help you make millions of dollars.

Having and working a good Top 25 *can be the single biggest driver of growth* for your business, but you have to work it right.

This is where that feeling of increase I talked about earlier comes in. The people in your Top 25 must believe that, because you are in their lives, they will get an increase, and that increase is so great that they want to help you get increase.

There must be real value added to these people's lives. You must not only give them the product or service, but you must give them "deep emotional support" and access to your networks (that are becoming much deeper due to your circulation).

I call this the TRIPLE VALUE:

- One, I give you my product or service and it is strong in its delivery.

- Two, I give you my "emotional support," meaning I feed you support and energy.

- Third, I give you access to my networks for you to exchange and expand with (See my book *Single Digit Millionaire* for more on this).

What this does is make these people huge fans of YOU. They are your biggest advocates. They are drinking your Kool-Aid, maybe even swimming in it. They are friends, they are customers and they promote you to others. They're in the marketplace telling other people how great you are.

Remember, someone in your Top 25 is much more than a promoter who has to be *asked* to say something positive about you. These people are ADVOCATES for you. They are "fighting for you" in the marketplace. They are "feeding you" new opportunity, new business, and new circles of influence.

Let me ask you this...

What if you could create 25 people that sent you three referrals per year? That's a total of 75 referrals from your Top 25. What would that do to your business? Who do you think you could get connected to? What would the quality of those referrals be?

If you answered those questions honestly, you see how powerful the Top 25 can be.

To build a world-class Top 25, you have to learn the art and practice of advocating for other people. You are there for them. You go the extra mile to be an asset to their lives. They are part of your deep, entrenched network, and you make them into rich and meaningful relationships. You attend their events, you have dinner with them, you help them through the difficult times of life. In other words, *you advocate for them so they advocate for you.*

More than just friends, though, these people must be *referral sources.* They must be able to send you referrals. How do you get them to do that? You love on these people and you stay constantly engaged. See them a minimum of four times per year, send them gifts, include them in your inner circle, be a valuable part of their lives.

There must be *follow-up* and *frequency* with this group of people. You must be in the "flow" of their lives and remain active in their mind, so they are constantly thinking about you. When they're constantly thinking about you, they are constantly referring you.

These people are your deepest referral partners. Love on these people. Care about these people. Expand these people's lives. Move a statistic in their lives and in their businesses.

When thinking about what to do with your TOP 25, think like this:

- These people are your VIPs - they get intimate access to everything you do.

- Have intimacy with these people - think private dinners, sporting events, back porch talks, and more.

- Be a key connector for these people - introduce them to other "people of increase."

- Always move a statistic in their businesses - think deeply about how you can help them solve their greatest problems.

- Be there for the biggest moments of their lives and the low moments of their lives. People *never* forget.

One of the most important skills you can learn is to advocate for other people - both online and off. If you want people to advocate for you in the world of social media, tweet them, include them in Facebook posts, comment on their Instagram and pull them into your inner circles where they feel like they're a part of your team.

When you build 25 deep advocates with whom you're nourishing and working on relationships, they will begin to send you opportunities. And they can only do that if you're at the top of their minds. You stay "top of mind" by advocating for them.

By the way, an advocate - someone in your Top 25 - is NOT a client that you never speak to. It's not an acquaintance or someone that you talk to occasionally. A true advocate is someone who is in your inner circle and you love on them and they love on you back. You send them business; they send you business. These are your biggest VIPs.

Start now by identifying who would be ideal to be in this group. They have to fit the above to be part of your Top 25. Don't put lukewarm people in your TOP 25, or those who are selfish and not good at advocating for you. Not only do you have to be an asset to them, they have to be an asset to you.

So as you build your Top 25, wake up every week and touch three of your advocates in a deep and meaningful way. Let them know you care about them, let them know you're there for them, put money into their pockets, and send them referrals.

Should you stop at 25?

Imagine having 50, 75, 100, or even 200 people out there, growing your brand, working on your behalf, sending you referrals. Imagine great people sending other great people to you. If that's happening, we are all winning together.

Go build and love on your Top 25 now.

CHAPTER 4

NET PROMOTERS

When I'm coaching people on the Legacy Selling System, I'm often asked, "Where's the easiest place to start?"

Based on years of working the system and coaching thousands to work it successfully, I can tell you the easiest place to start is with your *current customers*. Love on them and *transform* them to the point where they actively advocate for you. Where they actively go out into the marketplace and promote you and refer to you.

Fred Reichheld, author of the book *The Ultimate Question*, says there are three types of customers.

First, there is a passive customer. They neither love you nor dislike you, they're simply lukewarm towards you. Next, there is a detractor. These customers don't (or didn't) like doing business with you and they are actively criticizing you and hurting your position in the marketplace. Finally, there are promoters. Promoters are your advocates. They're the ones out there telling other people how great you are.

You can measure whether a customer is a passive, a detractor, or a promoter with a simple question: "On a scale of one to 10, how likely is it that you would recommend us/me/this company to a friend or colleague?" Anything less than a seven is a detractor while a seven or an eight is a passive. You want people saying they are a 9 or a 10. You want *promoters*.

Once we understand that we want our current customers to be promoters, we focus on one thing: Becoming an *immediate* asset to them. If we do that, they will run and tell other people how great we are.

Dan Sullivan says it best, "Referrability is when great people tell other great people how great you are." That's what you want.

Your goal is to take your prospects, move them through the Farm Club to become clients and then move them to Net Promoters. You do that by becoming an immediate asset, making and keeping commitments, and by bringing incredible energy to the equation.

How?

You make them money, you save them money, or you add focus, drive, and ambition to their lives. You bring future clarity to the relationship. You add these things to the equation and they compensate you for those services and begin to see you as an asset to them.

One of the biggest mistakes salespeople make is waiting to make someone a promoter. You NEVER want to wait.

Start pushing them with your energy *immediately* after they make a decision to buy from you. Let them know that you are on their team. You will be there to see this through to its logical conclusion. You will become a major asset to their lives. Do it quickly and do it immediately and don't wait. Let them know that they need you. Show them you're a "must have" versus a "nice to have."

Many people drop the ball with current customers which means they don't turn them into promoters, advocates, and referrers. And because they don't, they not only lose potential referrals, they also lose customers. They have to work so hard to go out and get a new customer because they thought everything ended when the sale was made. Don't fall into this trap!

Take this strategy, take both your new clients and your current base, reactivate that base, love on these people, add unique value to them, and they will tell other people how great you are. That is how you create a Net Promoter.

CHAPTER 5

CONNECTORS

Step five of the Legacy Selling System is about building Connectors. Connectors are people who have influence and can get you in front of more of the right people.

The Legacy Selling System is built around one thing: increasing the probability of sales by increasing your activity with the *right* people. People you know, people you love, people you care about, and people you believe you can help. The *only* reason someone would end up in your system (Hit List, Farm Club, Top 25, etc.) would be one thing: you want a relationship with them.

What makes Connectors special and unique is they have *influence*. Every city, every town, every industry has influential people that can move your ball down the field and get you in front of the right people. Connectors act like magnifiers and multipliers when it comes to building your network and filling your funnel.

Connectors create a bridge between you and the people you want to get in front of and on your Hit List. Often, we can't just pick up the phone and call a person and say, "I'd like to do business with you." We have to come in the side door, and that's exactly what Connectors help you do.

Here's a great, recent example. I first met Tim Storey, celebrity life coach from Hollywood, at the second 10X Growth Conference, a major conference for those interested in maximizing their lives, in Las Vegas. We had similar beliefs and had a nice exchange at dinner.

I followed-up with Tim to connect and form a partnership. Tim, a pastor in L.A., helped to get my book *The Accountable Church* to key leaders around the country. He may even help me break into television by being a guest celebrity coach on his TV show that he is working on.

This is the idea of the Connector: a person who can "connect" you with new possibilities you hadn't even imagined before.

These people can:

- Connect you to new *influence*

- Connect you to new *opportunity*

- Connect you to key *people*

- Connect you with their loyal *audiences*

- Connect you to new *ideas*

They will open doors for you that you can't get in on your own, some of which you didn't even know to knock on.

Each week I identify key connectors that I need to be "connecting with" to open new doors. In the old days, a key connection may have introduced you to one or two new opportunities. In today's Instagram world, one connection, one podcast, one stage, or one business relationship could introduce you to millions of new people.

Robert Greene, the author of *Mastery*, *48 Laws of Power*, and *The Laws of Human Nature*, got his start from one key connection after fumbling through life. This man, his Connector, said he would fund his writing career. This connection got Greene launched and helped him go on to be a best-selling author.

I believe we are all just one relationship away from a new season in our lives. To make that happen, you have to work to become that "person of interest" that is "connecting" with others on a weekly basis to open doors.

A key part of this equation to open these doors is that you need to become that person of increase I talked about earlier. You can't be a taker. You have to be a giver. You are helping to "connect" your Connectors to new possibilities as well; this is not a one-sided relationship.

Each week you want to spend time with two Connectors. People that can introduce you to "this person" and "that person" and who are movers and shakers. Spend time with them, love on them, and ask them to introduce you to other people you want a relationship with, and explain that you believe you can add value to their lives.

Seek out people who are the movers and shakers, the influencers. Get on their schedules, articulate your value, let them know you are the real deal and they will introduce you and open doors to places you could never get in on your own.

Start right now by identifying 10-20 relationships you need to be "optimizing" to open new doors. For example, right now, I'm working with several key partnerships who are connecting me to major opportunities around the world.

Your next big break could come from *one key connection*. Connection is part of the selling system. Work this strategy hard.

(Want to see how our Monster Producers are using the Connector strategy with each other and growing 43% or more in a full-year cycle? Reach out to my team at info@coachburt.com and they'll get you connected for a FREE audit.)

CHAPTER 6

CLIMBERS

Step six of the Legacy Selling System is to identify what I like to call Climbers. Climbers are people that go into two categories.

The first category is people that can't do business with you today for one (legitimate) reason or another, but can and want to at some point in the future. They say things to you like, "Let's talk again in six months," or "Come back to me when X or Y happens." Whenever you hear this, immediately put these people on your list of Climbers.

Because these people want to do business at some point but not today, they are different than your Farm Club.

The Farm Club is about *immediate* sales; the sales we're trying to get right *now*. You can think of Climbers as your "long-term Farm Club." Treat them with the same love, just know it's a future sales cycle.

The second category of Climbers is people who are on their way up in an organization. They are future movers and shakers and potential prospects when they get "there." Your job is to identify these people early in their ascent and say, "One day, I want a relationship with that person because they WILL be a BIG decision maker."

A great example of that was a few years ago. I had just gotten back from the University of Mississippi (Ole Miss), where, many years ago, I had built a relationship with a young aspiring assistant coach. I immediately identified him as a Climber. As time went on, he climbed through the ranks and became the recruiting coordinator at Kentucky, and I knew, one day, he would become a head coach and he would call me and say, "Coach, I want a relationship with you because you can be an asset to us." So I built the relationship over the years and loved on him. One day he gets there and we start doing business together. He was ready to become a person of interest and he needed me to make it happen.

Your objective is to identify the future stars that will be able to make decisions and/or buy from you at a point in the future. These are your Climbers and they are way too often overlooked.

Don't be the salesperson that overlooks them. Instead, identify two new Climbers each week. That'll give you 100 Climbers per year to go after, introduce yourself to, and demonstrate how you will be an asset to them in the future.

CHAPTER 7

ASPIRATIONAL CONTACTS

I believe big-time people need to be around other big-time people. Because of that, the Legacy Selling System has a concept called Aspirational Contacts.

For you, and the thousands of successful people using the Legacy Selling System, an Aspirational Contact is a person out in the world who is *really* good at what they do. You admire them, you respect them, you want to emulate them.

You can change the trajectory of your business and your life by spending time with one Aspirational Contact per week for a year. When you spend time with talent, it rubs off on you.

When you are low on motivation and spend time with motivated people, you become more motivated. When you're low on confidence and you spend time with confident people, you become more confident. You want to do things they're doing, and they *feed you energy*.

This Aspirational Contact could be someone in your community. It does not have to be a celebrity, a best-selling author, or a "who's who" in the world. It's just somebody that's really, really good.

How do you make it happen? It's easy. You call this

person, or you email him or her, and you say, "Hey, you're really good. I'd love to know how you became so good at what you're doing."

Most Aspirational Contacts will be more than happy to share, IF you listen and implement. You want to find out if they had pivot points in their lives. Did they have a breakthrough, did they have some sort of epiphany? Who did they study under? Most importantly, you're looking for *how can I be as good as you are?*

Doing this will feed your fire as a salesperson because it's simply impossible to become complacent when you're spending time with talent.

There's not always a substitute for one-on-one time with talent. Sometimes, though, you can gain impact and get credit by listening to a podcast, attending an event, or reading a book. When possible, always try to see them in person or hop on a Skype or Zoom call. Nothing can replace eyeball-to-eyeball time!

Every week you need to spend time with talent. It'll never let your flame burn out. You'll stay focused. You'll get better, you'll be more confident, and you'll continue to work your system.

(If you *really* want to up your Aspirational Contact game, reach out to us at info@coachburt.com and my team will walk you through how our Monster Producers are doing it.)

CHAPTER 8

THE SHOWCASE

This next part is the single best way to fill your funnel and put new leads on your Hit List. It's what I call the Showcase, and every salesperson and business owner needs to master it.

The Showcase is any opportunity, paid or not, for you to get in front of other people and share your message, share your vision, share what you do, and let them see YOU. Why? Because if I'm a prospect, here's what I know: If I'm turned on to you, then I'm open to hear what you have to say.

This is your chance to get in front of people and share your energy, your enthusiasm, your passion, your story, and what you believe.

What you're doing is "one-to-many," you're batching people together. Instead of knocking on doors one at a time, you can put 30, 40, 50, 100, or 1,000 or more in a room at once. And when you share your message in a group, it's multiplied, and so will the interest that's generated in you. From that interest, you'll generate leads, which means you're building your Hit List. Move those leads to prospects in your Farm Club and then on to clients who become Net Promoters. That's your job.

I believe that, if you're really good in front of people, The Showcase is possibly the best strategy you could ever use.

If you're a real estate agent, if you're a banker, if you're a salesperson, if you're an entrepreneur, seeking out opportunities for you to get in front of a group of people and sharing your message could be one of the greatest marketing tools you'll ever use.

The Showcase is an activation event for you to share what you've got with other people so they can be turned on to you and what you have. You *activate* them for you. When you do this, it dramatically increases your probability of selling. It gives you brand awareness and it could even be a massive brand driver if they like you enough.

Make sure you have some type of call to action and some take away for them. You don't want to be a star with no leads to show for it!

I want you to think of The Showcase in three ways:

1. There is an *Education* Showcase - an educational event you host such as workshops, seminars, dinners with speakers, etc.

2. There is an *Entertainment* Showcase - an event you create for people to socialize naturally around entertainment such as concerts, social exchanges, or sporting events. (A lot of business happens at these events).

3. There is an *"Edutainment"* or *"Entertrainment"* Showcase – where you provide edu-

cation and entertainment together. For example, you could take an educational event and add music (or wine) and you will see what I mean. These become exchanges of energy, especially when you combine music with education to create this environment.

I personally look for *any* reason to get in front of audiences. I know this is my best strategy that allows me to "showcase" my abilities.

This is why I prefer the speaking engagement so much. It allows me to "connect" with the audience and articulate my value. I want the audience to come to their own conclusion that I would be an asset to their lives and a conduit to their hopes and dreams. I believe there is no better strategy than The Showcase.

To secure showcase events I suggest you:

- Write your own book to have a *message* that you can share (Our Monster Publishing division can help you with this).

- Create and position by *power concepts* - meaning create great concepts that people care about. For example, if you're bringing people together to talk about long-term investing, I believe a concept around "Wealth Can't Wait" would be powerful.

- Bring unique people in to speak who have special skillsets that are attractive to your network. Doing this exponentially expands the value you offer.

One big mistake many people make is assuming you have to spend lots of money on The Showcase. That's not true. You just need a location and people. That location can come at a restaurant or your back patio.

Start now planning your next Showcase event, either for *suspects*, *prospects*, or *your clients* who you're working to turn into *advocates*.

Gather people together and watch how this energy is *activated.* Always, and I mean always, have something in the future to PUSH people toward (following the concept of a "Value Ladder" to start an upward cycle of engagement with you or another event).

Never waste an activation event to harness the energy of others and get people excited with "structures of exchange."

When you practice and use a Showcase event, you'll discover an unbelievable strategy to drive up leads, close more deals, and become a powerful person of interest.

(Interested in seeing me speak to see how our team does it? Email us at info@coachburt.com and we'll find a way.)

CHAPTER 9

THE DATABASE

You've created your Hit List, started working your Farm Club and Top 25, began building Net Promoters, and are focusing on Connectors and Climbers. You're also working on your Showcase strategy and spending time with Aspirational Contacts.

Now, it's time to leverage technology to build your lists and increase your sales. You'll do that through your Database.

Before we talk about your Database, here's some context and strategy for you. As I coach thousands on using the Legacy Selling System to grow their sales and business, I suggest practicing four primary strategies every 30 days. You then leverage two secondary strategies.

Your primary strategies might be your Hit List, Top 25, Farm Club, and a focus on Climbers.

When it comes to your secondary strategies, let's say you do a couple of Showcases of a month. And then you work your Database.

Your Database has the potential to be one of your biggest assets. It's your list of people who have given you their email addresses (or cell/text numbers) for you to follow-up with and stay in front of them. How you work your Database can be incredibly valuable to building a massive following of people.

Think of it this way: people of interest build engaged followers. They build a following of people who are drinking their Kool-Aid because they have something incredibly valuable. So when you're out there circulating and creating purposeful motion with the Legacy Selling System, collect email addresses everywhere you go. You want to pull people into your funnel and provide incredibly valuable content. That's your Database strategy.

Once a week you should be sending an email to your Database to add value.

For example, each week I talk about motivation, hidden assets, confidence, sales, leadership, management, and so on. I put a video in there as a tool and it is free to the people on my list. If they like what I've got, I invite them to something, whether it's a book, a bootcamp, my programs, or a speaking engagement. The point is, I always have a call to action - I always invite them to something in the future and let it build from there.

The key is to have something of value other people want so that they are willing to give you their email addresses and say, "I want to hear from you. I want some more of what you've got." Here's what I know about a following of people: you can monetize a following.

Think long-term: What if you had 10,000 people on your email list, 300,000 Twitter followers,

Facebook fans, and/or Instagram followers? What if you had all of these followers - your tribe - that you could consistently communicate with?

Build followers, add them to your Database, and work that Database. Get them drinking your Kool-Aid because, if they're drinking the Kool-Aid, the next thing they're going to do is pull out their wallets and spend some money with you. This is a great way to monetize the love.

(If you're not in my database receiving my emails, you're missing out! Email info@coachburt.com and my team will invite you along.)

NOW IS YOUR TIME

If you want to succeed in sales and business, you need to have a *real* customer-getting strategy. You must wake up and circulate with purpose every single day. Big-time people don't waste time and energy wandering around trying to figure out how to get customers; they work a system.

I believe those who work a system sell more and do better than those that don't. I've seen it myself and in the thousands that I coach each month, and that's why I created the Legacy Selling System to help YOU sell more and grow your business.

The Legacy Selling System gives you peace of mind so that, every week, you go to work with purpose, direction, focus, and clarity. You'll wake up with a system to get new customers and turn them into massive referral sources.

The system works. It's been proven by the thousands I've coached, but there's one catch. YOU have to work it; nothing works unless YOU do.

The Legacy Selling System takes you from chasing business to attracting it. It helps you be great so other people tell other people how great you are. It's about having an intentional strategy to dramatically increase your probability of selling.

I spend every day coaching and developing companies and talent just like YOU. If you want to know how we can help drive an increase of 43% or more in your business this year, reach out to my team at info@coachburt.com. We'll move mountains to help you win and become a person of interest.

Now is YOUR time!

ABOUT THE AUTHOR

Coach Micheal Burt is considered "America's Coach," a unique blend of a former championship basketball coach combined with a deep methodology of inner-engineering people to produce at a higher level in the business world.

Coach Burt has a simple philosophy: "Everybody needs a good coach in life" and believes those that have great coaches outperform and out-earn those that don't.

Coach Burt currently runs a multimillion-dollar coaching business and his world-wide coaching program, Monster Producer, which teaches the five big areas to get a significant lift of 43% or greater in your business.

Burt is an international speaker and personal coach to some of the top performing companies in the world.

CPSIA information can be obtained
at www.ICGtesting.com
Printed in the USA
JSHW030714050521
14327JS00003B/8